Blockchain

Joseph Todaro

CHERRY LAKE
Publishing

Published in the United States of America by Cherry Lake Publishing
Ann Arbor, Michigan
www.cherrylakepublishing.com

Reading Adviser: Marla Conn, MS, Ed., Literacy specialist, Read-Ability, Inc.

Photo Credits: ©LookerStudio/Shutterstock.com, cover, 1; ©WAYHOME studio/Shutterstock.com, 5; ©smolaw/Shutterstock.com, 6; ©Monkey Business Images/Shutterstock.com, 7; ©eclipse_images/iStock, 8; ©853creative/Shutterstock.com, 10; ©Rawpixel.com/Shutterstock.com, 13; ©Gusfikri Mahardika/Shutterstock.com, 14; ©Samuel Borges Photography/Shutterstock.com, 15; ©imagedepotpro/iStock, 17; ©PeopleImages/iStock, 19; ©skynesher/iStock, 20; ©Roman Pyshchyk/Shutterstock.com, 23; ©andersphoto/Shutterstock.com, 24; ©Asada Nami/Shutterstock.com, 26

Graphic Element Credits: ©Ohn Mar/Shutterstock.com, back cover, multiple interior pages; ©Dmitrieva Katerina/Shutterstock.com, back cover, multiple interior pages; ©advent/Shutterstock.com, back cover, front cover, multiple interior pages; ©Visual Generation/Shutterstock.com, multiple interior pages; ©anfisa focusova/Shutterstock.com, front cover, multiple interior pages; ©Babich Alexander/Shutterstock.com, back cover, front cover, multiple interior pages

Library of Congress Cataloging-in-Publication Data

Names: Todaro, Joseph Edward, author.
Title: Blockchain / by Joseph Todaro.
Description: Ann Arbor : Cherry Lake Publishing, [2019] | Series: Disruptors in tech | Audience: Grades: 4 to 6. | Includes bibliographical references and index.
Identifiers: LCCN 2019006015 | ISBN 9781534147584 (hardcover) | ISBN 9781534150447 (pbk.) | ISBN 9781534149014 (pdf) | ISBN 9781534151871 (hosted ebook)
Subjects: LCSH: Cryptocurrencies—Juvenile literature. | Blockchains (Databases)—Juvenile literature.
Classification: LCC HG1710 .T63 2019 | DDC 332.4—dc23
LC record available at https://lccn.loc.gov/2019006015

Printed in the United States of America
Corporate Graphics

Joseph Todaro has been investing in and writing about blockchain technology since 2013. He is currently a managing partner at a blockchain investment fund. He resides in Michigan.

Table of Contents

CHAPTER ONE

Introduction to Blockchain

Imagine for a moment a completely **digital** world. It only exists online. You have a house, cars, and many other belongings all within this digital world. You even have a job. You are paid for your work and can use that digital money to buy more digital items. However, in a digital world where any digital item can be generated online at no extra cost, because there is no real labor being done, what is it that you actually own? How can you prove which digital items belong to you? How can you protect them?

In the real world, this is a simpler task. We protect our property by storing it in our houses. We have paper documents or certificates that prove ownership. In the digital world, this is a much more challenging problem. How can you prove you actually own that song on iTunes or that movie on Amazon Prime? **Blockchain technology** may solve this problem.

In the digital world proving ownership can be difficult.

Each time ownership of an item is changed, a transaction is recorded to the blockchain.

Proof of Ownership

Think of the blockchain as a list of digital items. This list is called the blockchain **ledger**. This ledger tracks who owns each digital item. It is impossible for anyone to take or copy your digital item. You own it. When you send your digital item—like an e-book or online game—to a friend, a **transaction** is recorded on the blockchain ledger. This transaction is proof that you gave your e-book or online game to your friend. Now your friend owns that digital item. This ledger is always correct, and anyone can verify this ledger to make sure it is accurate.

Each transaction on the blockchain can be verified by anyone with an internet-connected device, like a smartphone or laptop.

Mining equipment produces a lot of heat and needs to constantly be cooled by fans.

Miners

But who maintains these ledgers and records these transactions to ensure accuracy? This is the job of "miners." They get their name from miners who dig for gold or silver. However, these miners do not use picks and shovels; instead, they use computers. When you send a digital item to your friend, a miner verifies that transaction on a computer. After it's verified, the miner adds the transaction to the blockchain ledger. Without the miners, we would not be able to keep track of these digital items, and the blockchain ledger would become inaccurate. Miners are very important. There are many miners all over the world adding transactions to the blockchain ledger to keep it up-to-date.

In addition to confirming transactions, miners also make sure the ledger is protected from any false changes. There are many reasons why someone might want to change the ledger. Maybe someone wants to take your digital item without paying you. They could try to change the ledger information and claim ownership of your item. This would be stealing. The miners help make sure nobody takes your digital property. The more miners there are, the more secure the ledger is.

Although the most popular blockchains today use miners, not all blockchains use them. Blockchains that use miners are called PoW (proof of work) blockchains. Blockchains that do not use miners are called PoS (proof of stake). These blockchains are secured by users "**staking**" their **digital assets**. Those digital assets being staked by these special users cannot be traded or spent on other things.

Warehouses like these exist all around the world and are filled with millions of dollars worth of mining equipment.

Protecting Digital Property

Miners use thousands of expensive, high-powered computers to protect digital property. There are large warehouses all over the world filled with specialized computers that make sure the blockchain ledger is accurate. The more computers there are, the more secure the ledger. These computers use a lot of electricity to provide this security. If added together, all the equipment used to secure the blockchain ledger uses as much electricity as a small country! This makes it really hard for anyone to falsely change the ledger and claim ownership of your digital property.

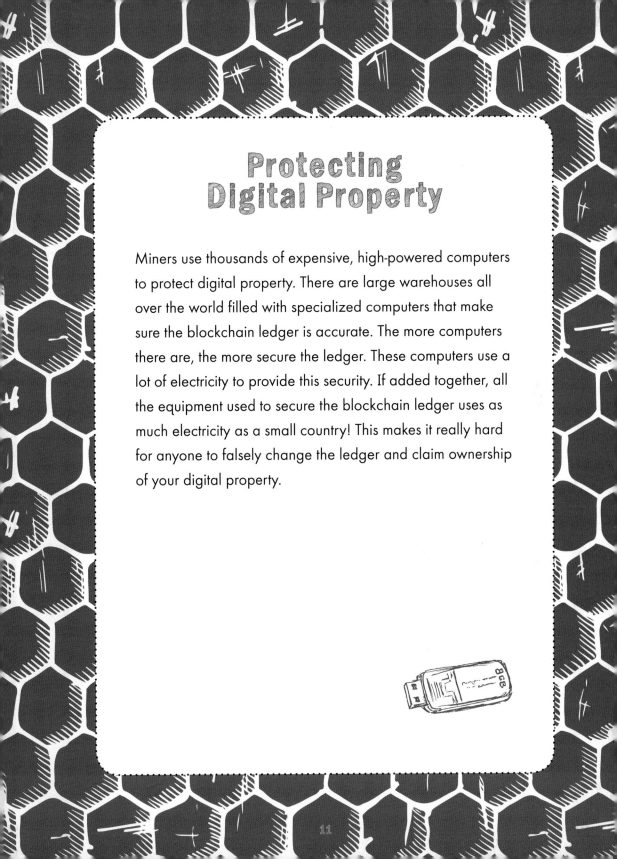

CHAPTER TWO

Digital Money

Now that we know the basics of blockchain technology, let's see how it is used today. What digital items are we talking about? The first digital item to use blockchain technology was digital currency, or money, called bitcoin. Before we explore digital money, we should first understand what we even mean by money.

What Is Money?

Money is anything that can be used as a form of payment. When you go to the store to buy a gallon of milk, you use money to pay for it. In the United States, the U.S. dollar is the main form of money. In other countries, other forms of money are used. Japan uses the Japanese yen. Many European countries use the euro. Some people even use gold or silver as a form of money.

Most countries around the world have their own money. The governments of those countries are responsible for issuing this money. They do this by printing it. Governments control how much new money is printed.

Money is anything that is used to pay for goods and services.

The bitcoin protocol has been coded so that there will only ever be 21 million bitcoin in existence.

Disrupting Money

Bitcoin is digital money that runs on a blockchain. It was created by people who wanted a different type of money, the kind that people could own and that could not be duplicated. Bitcoin is not controlled by anyone or any government. And it is impossible to print more bitcoin than what is coded into the blockchain program, which is also known as a protocol. The developers hoped all of this would allow bitcoin to become a global currency that could be used by everyone.

You can use bitcoin to buy many things, from cars and houses to food and clothes. There are many businesses that accept bitcoin. And you can send bitcoin to anyone in the world. All you need to send or receive bitcoin is a smartphone or laptop and a special online wallet. Many people in countries without reliable banks use bitcoin to send money to others and to buy things.

There are over 350,000 bitcoin transactions conducted everyday.

Some people think that bitcoin could disrupt the money we use today. They think that in the future, more people will use bitcoin instead of other forms of money like the U.S. dollar or Japanese yen.

Bitcoin is also an **investment**. The price of a bitcoin is constantly changing. The price depends on the demand. If many people want it, they buy more and the price goes up. When people do not want it anymore, they sell it and the price goes down. In the field of **economics**, this is called supply and demand. The supply and demand for bitcoin determines the price.

One of the earliest recorded bitcoin transaction was in 2010. It was for the purchase of two pizzas. Those two pizzas cost 10,000 bitcoin, or about $30 at the time. Bitcoin has gained in popularity since then, and now each bitcoin is worth a lot more money. Those 10,000 bitcoin today would be worth over $30 million. Those were expensive pizzas!

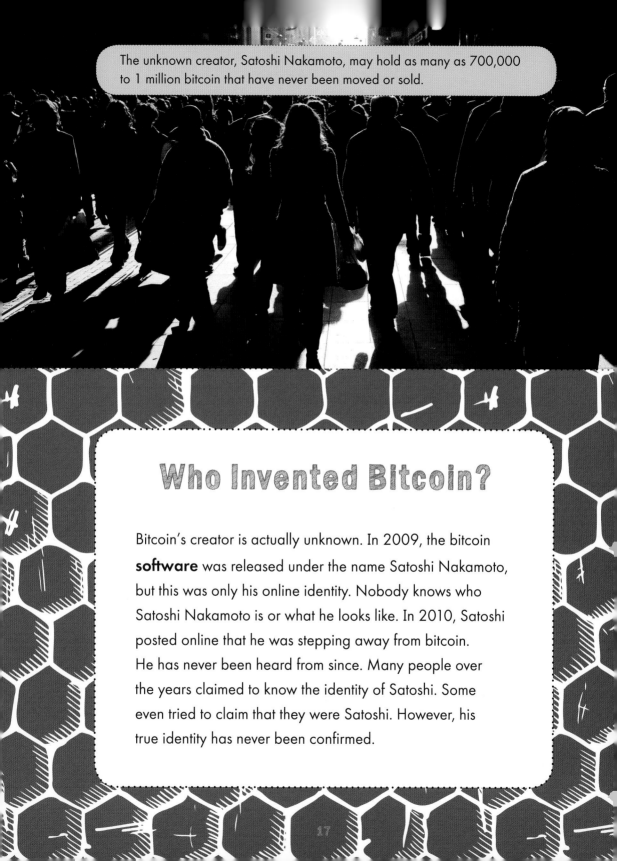

The unknown creator, Satoshi Nakamoto, may hold as many as 700,000 to 1 million bitcoin that have never been moved or sold.

Who Invented Bitcoin?

Bitcoin's creator is actually unknown. In 2009, the bitcoin **software** was released under the name Satoshi Nakamoto, but this was only his online identity. Nobody knows who Satoshi Nakamoto is or what he looks like. In 2010, Satoshi posted online that he was stepping away from bitcoin. He has never been heard from since. Many people over the years claimed to know the identity of Satoshi. Some even tried to claim that they were Satoshi. However, his true identity has never been confirmed.

CHAPTER THREE

Trust

Trust is a part of our everyday lives. When we order food, we trust that we will receive the meal we purchased. Similarly, when we send an online payment, we trust that our money will arrive as promised. If we sent $100 to a friend only to have $20 show up in her account, that would be bad.

Where We Put Our Trust

So who exactly are we trusting? We are trusting the businesses and people that provide these services. These businesses make sure that we get what we purchased. Some businesses hire other people to provide these services independently. This comes at a cost to the service provider and the customer. Because of this, the service can sometimes be very expensive. For example, popular ride-hailing **apps** like Uber and Lyft can take as much as a 25 percent fee from every ride just for connecting the riders and drivers! Eliminating the **middlemen** would allow people to save money. Middlemen are people or businesses that take a fee to help arrange an interaction between two or more people.

Middlemen are not needed in agreements that rely on smart contracts.

A More Trustworthy System

Smart contracts can help to eliminate the middlemen. A contract is a written agreement between two or more people. This agreement can be created for many different reasons.

Smart contracts are used to enforce agreed-upon rules between two or more people. They do this without ever requiring another person to intervene. This way you can trust that the agreement you made with your friend will not be broken.

Special companies, like auditing firms, are often hired to look over smart contracts to make sure there are no coding errors.

Imagine you gave your friend $20 to help buy a new online game. As part of the deal, you might ask that you be allowed to play the game just as much as your friend does. You could then get a lawyer to write up this contract. This contract would give you the right to play the game you helped buy. If your friend did not hold up his end of the deal, you could take him to court to get your money back.

A smart contract could remove the need for expensive lawyers and the court system for situations like these. This smart contract could be programmed to enforce the terms of the agreement. If your friend's online time is much greater than yours, the smart contract could automatically limit his play time and increase yours until you are even. This is much cheaper and faster than taking your friend to court to settle the disagreement.

Smart Contracts

Smart contracts are just lines of computer code. Smart contracts can also have "bugs" in them, just like any other computer program. Bugs are pieces of code that behave unexpectedly. When this happens, money can be lost. In 2016, a smart contract called "the DAO" was found to have bugs in it. Because of these bugs, a hacker was able to steal $150 million of other people's money. This was one of the biggest hacks of all time! Fortunately, most of the money was recovered.

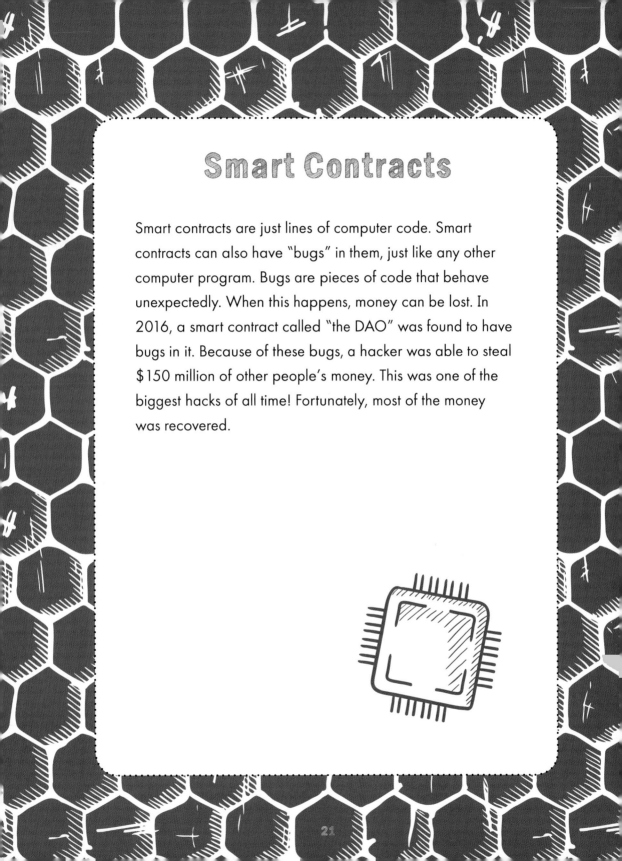

There are specialized devices that can securely store your digital assets. These are called hardware wallets.

The offshore banking industry is also being challenged by the blockchain. Offshore banks are banking services located in a country other than your own. These are often used by people who are looking to protect their money from local regulations or government action. The blockchain can be used to protect assets from both of these. For this reason, people all over the world store billions of dollars of wealth in blockchain assets.

Real Estate

The real estate industry is seeing benefits from blockchain technology as well. This industry involves a lot of paperwork that needs to be properly recorded. This process can be expensive and involve many people. The blockchain allows the simple tracking and recording of real estate transactions. The transfer of property rights could also be done securely and easily between two parties. All of this information is recorded to the blockchain and used to keep track of who owns which properties.

Health Care

While the health care industry is often slow to implement new technology, it could benefit from the blockchain as well. Whenever you visit the doctor, you generate what is called health data. This is information regarding your health. Health data remains fragmented and difficult to share. This process is inefficient. Moving patient data and physician interactions onto the blockchain could allow a more efficient and low-cost method of tracking and sharing patient health information.

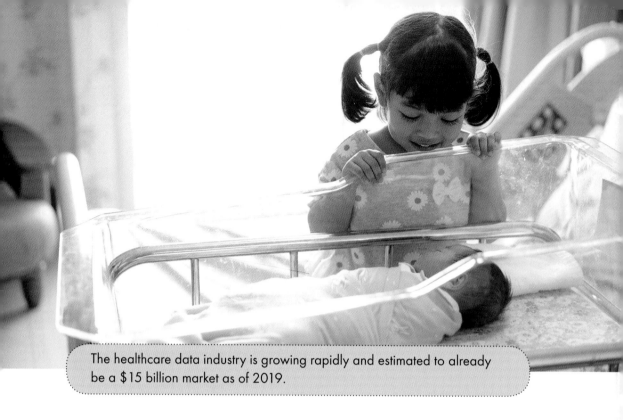

The healthcare data industry is growing rapidly and estimated to already be a $15 billion market as of 2019.

This method of storing and sharing health information could also allow patients to have control over their own health data. Your health data is very valuable to many companies. They pay a lot of money for your data. Currently, patients do not own their health data and so cannot benefit from its use. This could change with the use of the blockchain where patients are free to earn money from sharing their data or choose to keep it private altogether.

The future of blockchain is promising. While there are many uses of the blockchain that are being explored today, it is still very early in its development. Over the coming years, there will be more advances made to this young technology. Many of the ways in which blockchain will be used in the future probably have not even been discovered yet!

Sending Money Across the Globe

Many people go to other countries for work opportunities and then send money back home to their families. This is called remittance. Workers around the world send as much as $450 billion back to their families every year. Banks often charge high remittance fees for this service. The transfer of money also happens slowly. After the high transfer fees are paid to banks, the families receive a lot less than they would have. Without these fees, workers could get more of their money to their families to help support them. There are several blockchain businesses that offer this service today.

Timeline

2009
Blockchain is introduced via bitcoin as the first decentralized money. Only a handful of people even know bitcoin exists.

2013
Hundreds of other blockchains are launched. Many people build their own blockchains using the Bitcoin codebase.

2012
The popular bitcoin exchange Coinbase is created. This exchange is used to trade bitcoin and other blockchain assets. As of 2019, Coinbase employs over 500 people and is valued at more than $8 billion.

2013

The Ethereum blockchain is created, popularizing the idea of smart contracts. It is built in part by the then 20-year-old college dropout, Vitalik Buterin. In 2018, it is worth more than $15 billion.

2017

Thousands of blockchain projects and applications are launched. Many of these were launched through ICOs (initial coin offerings), an alternative method for young projects to raise investment money.

2014

Mt. Gox, the largest bitcoin exchange at the time, collapses after a hack. Nearly $500 million worth in bitcoin is allegedly stolen.

Learn More

Books

Anderson, Rane. *Cryptography.* Huntington Beach, CA: Teacher Created Materials, 2017.

Coding and Computers. Minneapolis, MN: Discovery Kids, 2016.

Websites

Blockchain for Kids
https://lisk.io/academy/blockchain-basics/blockchain-for-kids
Discover more about how blockchain records information safely and securely.

Youtube—What is Bitcoin? (for kids)
https://youtu.be/nqdv6Ad9Nt4
Learn the basics of bitcoin and cryptocurrencies from the perspective of the "CryptoCoinKid."

Glossary

apps (APS) applications downloaded to a mobile device

autonomous (aw-TAH-nuh-muhs) acting independently

blockchain (BLAHK-chayn) a digital ledger that records transactions

decentralized (dee-SEN-truh-lized) distributing control or power from a central group to a wider group

digital (DIJ-ih-tuhl) relating to computer technology

digital assets (DIJ-ih-tuhl AS-ets) the currency of any given blockchain

economics (ee-kuh-NAH-miks) area of study concerned with the production, consumption, and transfer of wealth

investment (in-VEST-mint) spending money in the hopes of gaining more profit

ledger (LEJ-ur) a recorded list of information

middlemen (MID-uhl-men) people who arrange business deals between others

smart contracts (SMAHRT KAHN-trakts) self-executing agreements that require no middlemen

software (SAWFT-wair) programs and related information used by a computer

staking (STAYK-ing) the act of holding digital assets in order to gain rewards and/or secure a PoS blockchain network

technology (tek-NAH-luh-jee) use of science to solve problems

transaction (tran-SAK-shuhn) an exchange or interaction between people

Index